simply wood

simply wood

Home Projects from Branches, Logs, and Other Found Wood

Linda Suster

**STACKPOLE
BOOKS**

Guilford, Connecticut

STACKPOLE
BOOKS

Published by Stackpole Books
An imprint of The Rowman & Littlefield Publishing Group, Inc.
4501 Forbes Blvd., Ste. 200
Lanham, MD 20706
www.rowman.com

Distributed by NATIONAL BOOK NETWORK
800-462-6420

Editorial Director: Ellen Dupont
Senior Editor: Julie Brooke
Editor: Dorothy Stannard
Designer: Leah Germann
Text and Principal Photography: Linda Suster
Index: Marie Lorimer

British Library Cataloguing in Publication Information available

Library of Congress Cataloging-in-Publication Data available

ISBN 978-0-8117-3858-3 (paperback)
ISBN 978-0-8117-6855-9 (e-book)

♾️™ The paper used in this publication meets the minimum requirements of American National Standard for Information Sciences—Permanence of Paper for Printed Library Materials, ANSI/NISO Z39.48-1992.

Contents

Introduction

Growing up on the Big Island of Hawai'i, I began collecting shells, driftwood, and other natural knickknacks from an early age. Whenever wood washed up, I always liked to imagine the life it had led before reaching me. Moving to southern California in my early teens, I found driftwood on this new shore had a personality of its own. A wondrous array of different shapes, colors, and textures introduced a whole new world to me! Once I had a family, I began an annual tradition of taking a weeklong summer vacation from our home in sunny San Diego County to beautiful Lake Tahoe in northern California. Driving a different route each year allowed us to explore new riverbanks, lakeshores, and coastlines.

This hobby of collecting unique twigs, branches, rocks, and shells led to creating presents for family and friends. Their reactions inspired me to produce my projects on a larger scale! Since then, I've spent countless hours scouring the shores of lakes and oceans (where it is legal to take such items), or hunched over a piece, gluing in the tiniest detail. I've loved every second of creating items that have become the cherished possessions of others.

Nearly all of the wood featured in this book was handpicked on my travels, and each piece holds a special memory of where I found it. Use pieces you've collected over the years to make the projects for yourself. Some techniques take more practice than others, and I know from experience how intimidating it can be to learn a new skill. Rest assured, the book is full of useful tips and easy-to-follow steps to keep you headed in the right direction. Just be sure to give yourself enough time to complete each of the steps. And, as with cooking, once the fire's hot, there's no time to waste, so be sure you have everything at hand before you begin.

Once you have tried a few things, don't be afraid to put your own spin on a project! My way is definitely not the only way, and if something feels more comfortable and seems like it's going to work, go for it! Best of luck, and happy creating.

Linda

Linda

Twig

The Twig Vase on page 10 proves that even
the smallest twig can be transformed
into something useful for the home.
Larger twigs can be cut into lengths
and threaded together to become a
Christmas-tree-shaped work of art,
while a single sturdy twig supports
a tinkling row of glass chimes.

Twig Vase

With four components and minimal tools, you'll build this woodland-themed vase in no time! The twigs hide a glass vase, which holds the water and flower stems.

MATERIALS

28–32 twigs, 5½ in. (14cm) long

1 length of twine, 16 in. (40.5cm) long

1 length of raffia ribbon, 40–48 in. (101.5–122cm) long

Jar, 5½ in. (14cm) tall and 3½ in. (9cm) in diameter

TOOLS

Ruler

Drill with drill bit large enough to make a hole the diameter of the twine

Scissors

TIP
Choose a selection of twigs in different shades or colors. They should be relatively straight and smooth so they fit snugly against each other in a row. As they are decorative, they do not need to be sturdy, but they must be thick enough to drill through.

Twig Vase

1 Use a ruler to measure the center of the length of each twig and drill a hole through the twigs at that point.

2 Decide on the order of the twigs, then thread the twine through the holes.

3 Arrange the twigs around the sides of the vase then tie the twine in a tight double knot (see page 120) to secure them. Cut the excess twine.

4 Wrap the raffia ribbon around the vase so that it hides the twine and tie in a double knot and then in a bow. Trim the ends of the ribbon to neaten them.

DESIGN IDEA

We decorated this vase with a rustic, raffia ribbon rather than the colorful red one on page 11. You can choose a bright or a neutral color, or change the ribbon to suit your mood, the season, or the flowers.

Twig Christmas Tree

Use this fun, festive tree to display your favorite ribbons and baubles. You'll be able to use it year after year to celebrate the season and bring a splash of holiday cheer to your front door.

MATERIALS

Approximately 16 twigs of various sizes, 2½ in. (6.3cm) to 16 in. (40.5cm) long

Wooden star, 3 in. (7.6cm) wide

2 lengths of twine, 72 in. (182.8cm) long

1 length of twine, 18 in. (45.7cm) long

Spools of yellow, blue, and red ribbon, ¼ in. (0.5cm) wide

Spool of turquoise ribbon, ⅜ in. (1cm) wide

Holiday decor such as ornaments, bells, foliage, and berry clusters

TOOLS

Band saw or strong pruning shears

Ruler

Scissors

Glue gun with glue sticks

Twig Christmas Tree

1 On a flat surface arrange the twigs in a triangle, with the shortest at the top and the longest at the base. If necessary, adjust the lengths using a band saw or strong pruning shears. Use the 72 in. (182.8cm) length of twine to tie the twigs together along one side, starting at the top and being sure to evenly space the pieces (see Tip, below). Repeat on the other side.

2 Tie the ends of the string at the base of the tree to secure them using a double knot (see page 120). Cut off the excess string.

3 Use the 18 in. (45.7cm) length of twine to tie the wooden star to the top of the tree using a double knot.

TIP
To tie the twigs together, wind one end of the twine around the top twig and tie a double knot (see page 120). Repeat for each twig until you reach the base. The twigs will look like a ladder.

4 Tie a bow around the star using the turquoise ribbon.

5 Tie lengths of the ribbons into bows, and use a glue gun to attach them and the other decor to the tree to create a balanced and festive effect.

TIP

If your star decoration has a hanger, you can use this to hang the tree. Alternatively, you can buy a hanger and glue it to the back of the star.

Fish
Wind Chime

Enjoy the sound of passing breezes tinkling through this nautical-themed wind chime. We have used glass fish to decorate it, but you can use any shape you like. Just make sure that the pieces of glass hang at an even length so that they knock against each other.

MATERIALS

11 in. (28cm) piece of driftwood, about 1 in. (2.5cm) thick

12 glass wind chime fish (available online)

12 lengths of twine, 8–10 in. (20.3–25.4cm) long

Length of twine, 12–14 in. (30.5–35.5cm) long

TOOLS

Ruler

Pencil

Drill with drill bit large enough to make a hole the diameter of the twine

Scissors

Fish Wind Chime

1 Using the ruler and pencil, mark twelve points about ¾ in. (2cm) apart along the length of the piece of driftwood. Drill a hole at each point.

2 Tie the twelve shorter lengths of twine to the glass fish using a double knot (see page 120), making sure they will hang evenly.

3 Thread the free end of each length of twine through one of the holes in the driftwood and secure with double knot (see page 120).

TIP
You can use as many, or as few, fish as you wish, just adjust the spaces between the holes so that they are an even distance apart. You can also adjust the lengths of the pieces of twine the fish hang from.

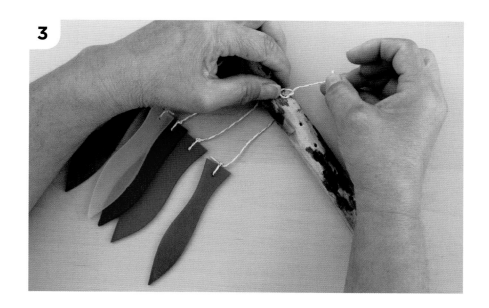

4 Drill a hole between the first and second knot on each end of the piece of driftwood.

5 Thread the longer length of twine through the top of each hole and knot at the bottom. Hang the wind chime from this piece of twine.

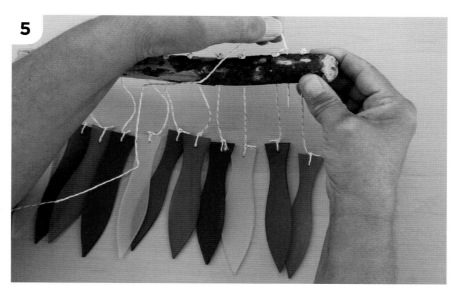

DESIGN IDEA

Instead of fish, look for other glass shapes online. Alternatively, string shells with holes drilled into them to create a wind chime fit for a mermaid. (For tips on drilling holes in shells, see page 53.)

Branch

Branches, whether thick and gnarled, straight, or curving, provide many options for creativity. A single gnarled branch supports a trio of coat hooks while a row of sturdy branches set into a frame gives you a place to hang your hat. Entwined with twinkling lights, a cluster of branches becomes a rustic chandelier.

Trio of Coat Hooks

Look for a branch with an intriguing shape that is large and sturdy enough to hold three metal coat hooks. The finished piece will add rustic charm to a hallway.

MATERIALS

Branch (size will depend on preference and availability)

Sawtooth hanger

3 coat hooks with screws

TOOLS

Hand planer, if required

Drill

Pencil

Trio of Coat Hooks

1 If the back of the branch needs to be flattened to enable it to sit flush against the wall, use a hand planer to smooth the surface.

2 Attach the hanger to the back of the branch by following the package instructions.

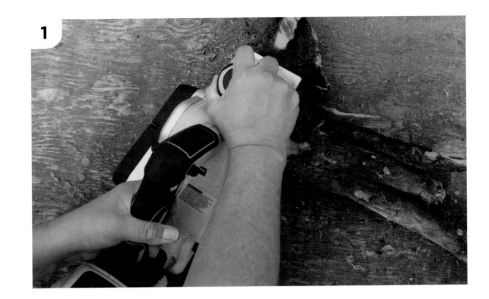

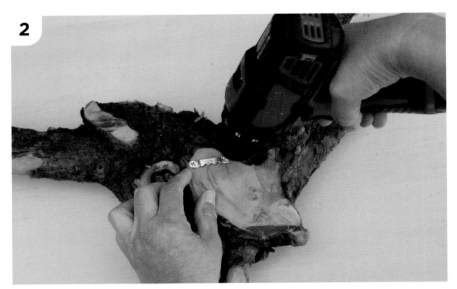

TIP

When using a planer, always remember to go "with the grain," as you would when sanding. For more tips on planing, see page 114.

3 On the front of the branch, use a pencil to mark the desired locations of the coat hooks. Make a pencil mark for the position of each screw required to hold the hooks in place.

4 Drill pilot holes at the marked locations.

5 Use the screws provided to secure the hooks to the branch. Attach the coat rack to the wall using the hanger.

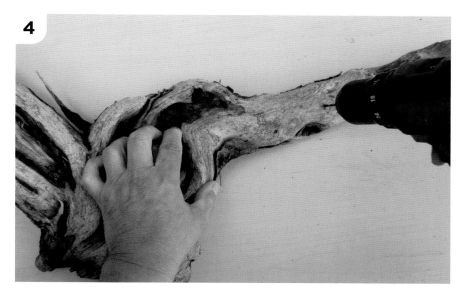

Branch Chandelier

Bring a little bit of the forest into your home and add a touch of whimsy to any dinner party with this simple chandelier. The branches that make up this chandelier hang from a metal ring and are decorated with a string of sparkly, battery-operated lights.

MATERIALS

4–5 branches, 30–36 in. (76–91.5cm) long

Battery-operated LED string lights, with batteries

Metal ring, 2 in. (5cm) diameter

6–8 ft. (1.8–2.4m) of rustic-looking rope

Two lengths of small gauge, bendable wire, 14–16 in. (35.5–40.5cm) and 36 in. (91.5cm) long

TOOLS

Brush

Pruning shears

Scissors

Wire cutting pliers

Branch Chandelier

1 Use the brush to clean any debris or loose pieces from the branches. Arrange the branches so that they fit together at the bases and flare out at the tips.

2 Use a pair of pruning shears to remove any excess twigs from the bottom 6 in. (15cm) of the branches so that they will fit together closely at the base.

3 Use the shorter length of wire to secure the battery pack for the lights to the base of one of the branches by wrapping it around and through the pack. Make sure that the on/off switch on the pack remains accessible.

4 Cluster the other branches around the branch with the battery pack attached so that the ends flare out. Tie the branches together at the base using the longer length of wire, being careful to keep the battery pack on the outside of the cluster.

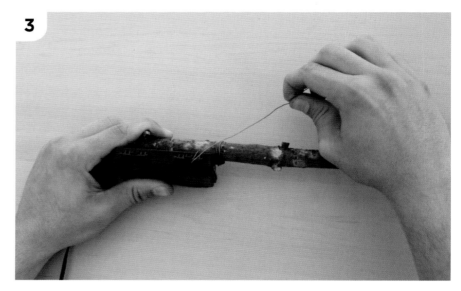

5 Tie the length of rope around the metal ring and secure with a double knot (see page 120). Insert one branch into the ring.

6 Wedge the rope knot through the center of the cluster of branches and tighten it. Then wrap the rope around the cluster to hide the battery pack, making sure you can still access the on/off switch.

7 Tie a double knot at the top of the chandelier close to the ring to secure everything in place.

8 Arrange the lights on the chandelier so that the lights are distributed throughout the branches.

TIP
You may need a second pair of hands to help you to stabilize the chandelier while you insert the branch and rope into the ring in step 5.

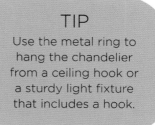

TIP
Use the metal ring to hang the chandelier from a ceiling hook or a sturdy light fixture that includes a hook.

Rustic Coatrack

Your houseguests are sure to love this rustic coatrack, a great addition to any hallway! Use branches that are at least 1 in. (2.5cm) in diameter so that they are sturdy enough to hold coats and bags, as well as hats and the dog's leash.

MATERIALS

7 sturdy twigs, at least 12 in. (30.5cm) long

2 pieces of reclaimed wood, 12 x 3 in. (30.5 x 7.6cm)

2 pieces of reclaimed wood, 30 x 3 in. (76.2 x 7.6cm)

Twenty-two ¾ in. (2cm) #6 screws

2 sawtooth hangers with screws

TOOLS

Heavy-duty pruning shears

Miter saw

Drill with drill and screwdriver bits

Rustic Coatrack

1 Use the heavy-duty pruning shears to trim the twigs so they are all 12 in. (30.5cm) long. Arrange them on a flat surface in the desired order.

2 On a flat surface, arrange the pieces of reclaimed wood to create a rectangular frame that will fit the twigs. Secure the pieces of wood together at the corners, using two screws at each corner. There is no need to drill pilot holes.

TIP
Use branches that are from the same type of tree and at least 1 in. (2.5cm) thick with lots of smaller branches coming off them to make the "rack" spots. One way to achieve this is to find a long branch and cut it into 12 in. (30.5cm) pieces.

3 Arrange the twigs inside the frame so that they are at the front edge and spaced evenly. Secure the twigs to the frame using a screw at each end of each twig. There is no need to drill pilot holes.

4 Decide on the position of the sawtooth hangers—as they will bear the weight of the coatrack they should be about 1–1½ in. (2.5–3.8cm) in from each edge. Drill pilot holes into the back of the frame, then secure the hangers with screws.

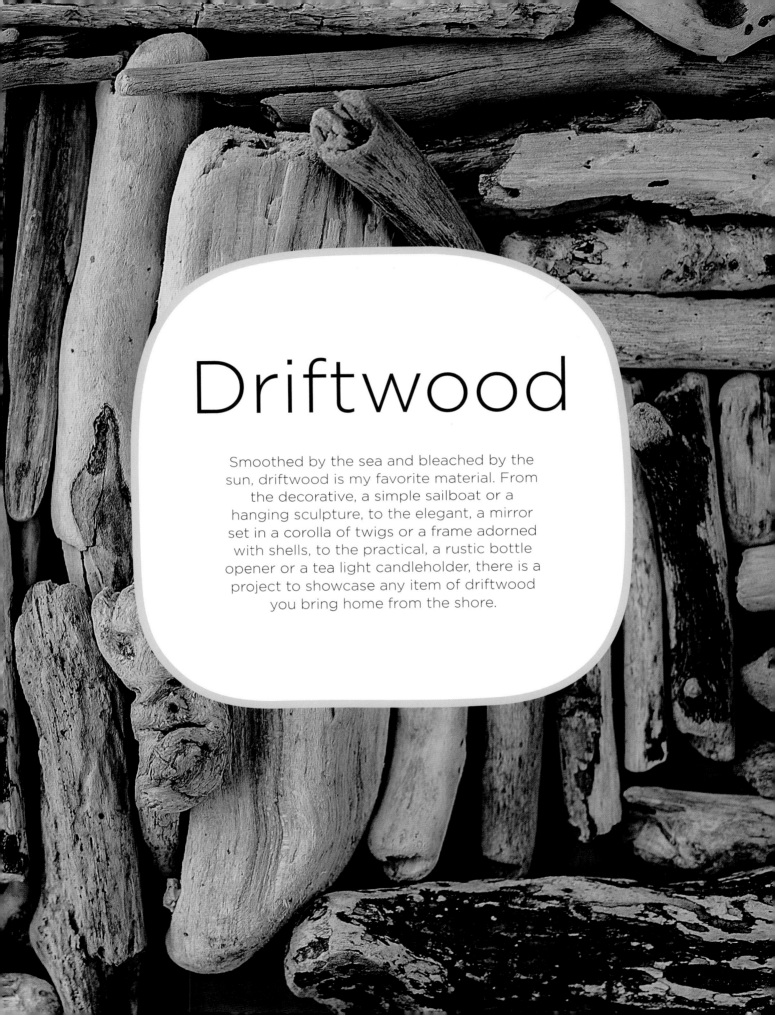

Driftwood

Smoothed by the sea and bleached by the sun, driftwood is my favorite material. From the decorative, a simple sailboat or a hanging sculpture, to the elegant, a mirror set in a corolla of twigs or a frame adorned with shells, to the practical, a rustic bottle opener or a tea light candleholder, there is a project to showcase any item of driftwood you bring home from the shore.

Sunburst Wall Mirror

This beautiful statement piece with its sunburst design makes an eye-catching centerpiece for any wall. You can use driftwood for this project, but as you need one hundred pieces, you may find it easier to source suitable twigs.

MATERIALS

12 in. (30.5cm) particle board floral craft ring

Brown paint, or the color of your choice

About one hundred thick, 5–6-in-long. (12.5–15cm) twigs

10 in. (25.4cm) diameter mirror

Sawtooth hanger with accompanying screws

TOOLS

Paintbrush

Strong multipurpose craft glue

Drill with bit for sawtooth hanger

DESIGN IDEA

To make the piece even more dramatic, add a ring of driftwood pieces around the mirror. Lay the finished piece faceup on a work surface and arrange the pieces to make a circular frame. Glue them using the technique for the Shabby Chic Candleholder (see page 54).

Sunburst Wall Mirror

1 Paint the particle board ring and let dry.

2 Arrange a base layer of pieces of wood around the ring, aligning one end of each piece of wood with the inside edge of the frame. When you are happy with their positions, secure the pieces of wood with glue. Let dry.

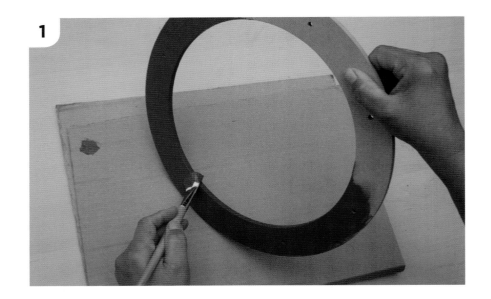

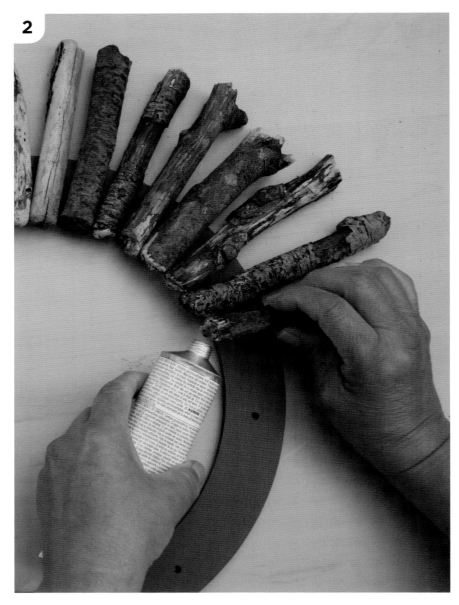

TIP
Instead of using a floral craft ring as the base for this mirror, you could use a rectangular, heart-shaped, or other frame.

3 Glue a second layer of wood on top of the base layer to add depth and texture. Position the pieces of wood between the pieces on the first layer. Let dry. Arrange a ring of twigs around the central hole in the frame. Let dry.

4 Carefully lay the twig frame facedown on a clean work surface. Position the mirror so that the glass is facedown and centered in the middle of the frame. Glue in place and let dry.

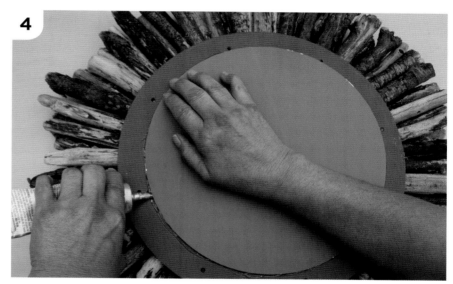

5 Decide where you want the top of the frame to be and add the sawtooth hanger at the top by attaching it to the particle board ring. To do this, drill two shallow pilot holes, then insert the screws. Hang the mirror on the wall.

DESIGN IDEA

The frame can be used without a mirror to make a stunning wall hanging.

Miniature Sailboat

Keep your memories of life at the beach—or on the water—alive by displaying this cute sailboat in your home. Even if you live far from the shore, it will be a daily reminder of sunny days with the wind in your hair and maybe the sand between your toes.

MATERIALS

1 flat piece of driftwood, 7–9 in. (17.8–22.8cm) long and 4–5 in. (10–12.5cm) wide

1 piece of ⅜ in. (1cm) wooden dowel, 12 in. (30.5cm) long

1 piece of patterned fabric, 8½ x 11 in. (21.6 x 28cm)

1 length of ribbon, approximately 4 in. (10cm) long

2 bronze furniture tacks, or similar wood screws with a head or hook to secure twine around

1 length of twine, approximately 48 in. (122cm) long

TOOLS

Pen

Ruler

Scissors

Piece of scrap wood or corkboard to use as a drilling base

Drill with a drill bit the same size as the dowel you're using

Large-eyed needle

Damp kitchen towel or cotton-tipped swab

Fabric glue

Wood glue

Miniature Sailboat

1 Fold the fabric in half on the diagonal to make a triangle. Use a pen and ruler to mark a straight line along the diagonal fold. Cut the fabric in half along the marked line.

2 Place the pieces of fabric on a work surface with the wrong sides toward you and the long vertical edges touching, so that they form a triangular sail. Place the length of dowel along the join in the fabrics to create the mast, leaving a small space at the top and 2½ in. (6.3cm) of the dowel exposed at the base. Apply glue to the central part of the dowel, leaving the top and bottom bare. Fold both pieces of fabric over the dowel and press to seal. Let dry completely.

3 Fold the length of twine in half to find the center and position the top of the dowel in the fold. Wrap the twine around the top of the dowel at the tip of the fabric sail, and tie a double knot (see page 120) to secure it.

4 Now wrap both ends of the twine twice around the dowel, wrapping on either side of the knot. Leave enough twine at each end to secure at the back of the dowel using a double knot.

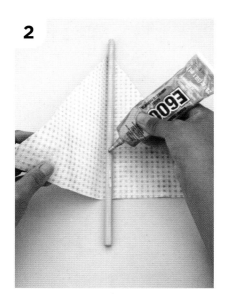

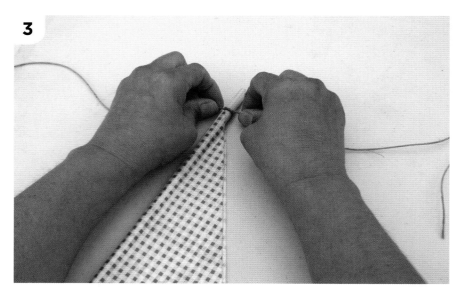

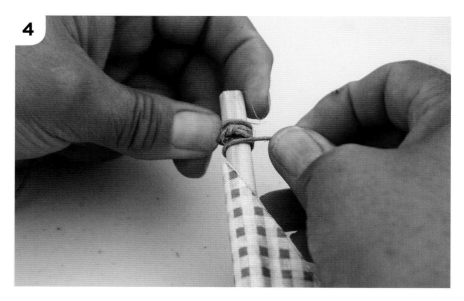

5 Thread one end of the twine through a large-eyed needle and stitch through the open edge side of the sail, creating six evenly spaced running stitches. Leave the other piece of twine free at the top of the sail.

6 Drill a shallow hole ½–¾ in. (1.3–2cm) deep and the diameter of the dowel, 2–3 in. (5–7.6cm) from one end of the piece of driftwood. Place a generous drop of wood glue into the drilled hole, insert the dowel, wipe away the excess glue using a damp cloth or cotton-tipped swab, and let dry completely.

7 Insert a furniture tack into the center of each end of the driftwood base so that it is secure but still protrudes from the wood.

8 Wrap the free end of one of the lengths of twine around one of the tacks as many times as needed to keep it taut. Add a dab of fabric glue to secure. Repeat with the end of the other length of twine and the second tack.

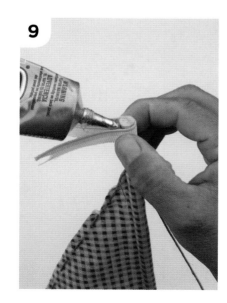

9 Fold the length of ribbon in half and cut a V shape into the cut ends. Wrap it around the top of the dowel, above the sail, and glue it in place. Let dry completely.

Seaside Mirror

Whimsical and beachy, this mirror will bring
a touch of the seashore into your home.

MATERIALS

8 x 10 in. (20.3 x 25.4cm)
rectangular mirror

Two 6–8 in. (15–20.3cm) pieces of
driftwood

Two 10–12 in. (25.4–30.5cm)
pieces of driftwood

Two 14–16 in. (35.5–40.5cm)
pieces of driftwood

8–10 shells

TOOLS

Strong multipurpose craft glue

Ruler

Seaside Mirror

1 On a work surface, place the two 14–16 in. (35.5–40.5cm) pieces of driftwood parallel to each other 7½ in. (19cm) apart with the right sides facing up.

2 Arrange the two 10–12 in. (25.4–30.5cm) pieces of driftwood at the ends of the longer pieces to create a frame. Secure with glue.

3 Arrange the two 6–8 in. (15–20.3cm) pieces of driftwood on the longer, vertical sections of the frame as desired. Secure with glue.

4 Arrange the shells on the frame as desired and secure in place with glue. Let the glue dry completely before proceeding to the next step.

5 Gently turn the frame over and lay it facedown on the work surface. Add a thin line of glue to each vertical interior edge of the wood (only the parts that will touch the mirror) and lay the mirror facedown onto the wood and so that it is centered. Press into place to ensure the glue is in contact with all the surfaces. Let dry completely before turning over and using.

DESIGN IDEA

Instead of inserting a mirror you can use the frame to hold a favorite photograph. Simply attach a magnetic clip frame to the back using a strong multipurpose craft glue. Then you can change the photograph if you wish.

Driftwood Sculpture

For this project, you can use a selection of found objects—driftwood, a shell, or even a length of rope, if you're lucky! If not you can purchase some additions. Either way, you're sure to make a sculpture that's perfect no matter where you hang it!

MATERIALS

40 to 60 pieces of driftwood, 4-5 in. (10-12.5cm) long

Length of rope, 36-48 in. (91.5-122cm) long

1 to 3 beads or 1 shell, depending on how you want to hang and finish the sculpture

TOOLS

Pencil

Piece of scrap wood or corkboard to use as a drilling base

Drill with drill bit the same size as the rope you're using

Brush

Scissors

Strong multipurpose craft glue

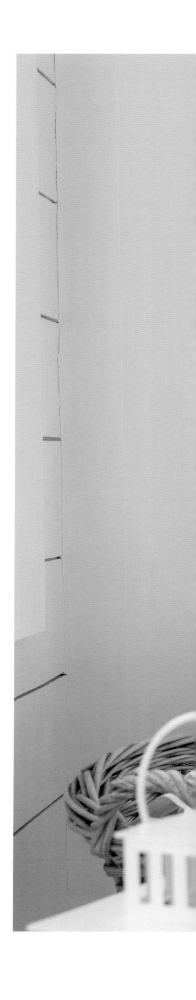

Driftwood Sculpture

1 Arrange all the pieces of wood in a row and decide on their order for the sculpture. Measure each one and mark the central point with a pencil.

2 Using the scrap wood or corkboard as a base to protect your work surface, drill a hole through each piece of wood and remove any debris with a brush.

TIP

You can measure the central point of each piece of wood—or simply estimate it. If you choose not to measure the wood, the finished sculpture will look more organic.

3 Prepare the rope. You can simply make a loop to hang the sculpture from (as here), or you can knot it around a bead or through a hole drilled in a shell (see Tip, below) using a double knot (see page 120).

4 String the rope through the pieces of wood, keeping them in the desired order—you can choose to make it as taut or loose as you'd like.

5 Once all the pieces are on the rope together, make sure the sculpture is at the desired tautness, then tie off the bottom in a double knot. Add some dabs of glue in the folds of the knot to secure it.

TIP

If you're using shells as well as twigs, be careful as you drill into them. Some shells, such as sand dollars and sea stars, are delicate and won't require very much pressure to drill, while others, such as a quahog, are extremely strong and thick and will take patience to break through!

Shabby Chic Candleholder

Instantly add rustic charm to any table setting with this tea light candle decoration. Small pieces of driftwood are arranged so that they hold a glass candleholder. We finished ours with a votive candle, but you can choose any candle you have at hand that fits your glass.

MATERIALS

10 to 15 driftwood pieces of varying sizes ranging from 3 in. (7.6cm) to 6 in. (15cm) long

Small glass votive candleholder

Small votive candle

TOOLS

Pencil

Cotton-tipped swab and damp paper towel (optional)

Strong multipurpose craft glue

Shabby Chic Candleholder

1 Arrange the pieces of wood in a tapered tower with the largest pieces crisscrossing each other to form the base, and the smaller, more curved pieces at the top to hold the glass candleholder. Make sure the hole in the center of the top layer is large enough to fit the candleholder but small enough to hold it firmly.

2 When you are happy with the arrangement of the pieces, make a pencil mark at the point of best contact between each one.

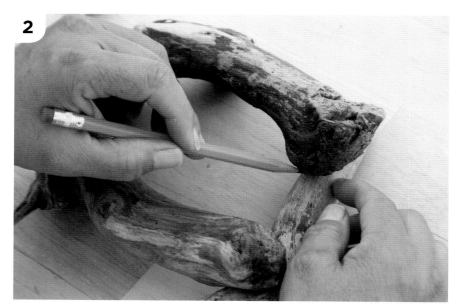

SAFETY

Before gluing the last layer of the wood, make sure the top of the glass candleholder will sit above the wood so there is no danger of the wood catching fire.

3 Take apart the tower, making a note of where the pieces go. Starting with the first layer, carefully add a dab of glue on each pencil mark. Join the pieces together and set aside for 20 to 30 minutes, or until the glue has dried, before assembling the next layer.

4 Repeat step 3 for each layer of wood.

5 The last layer needs to be tight enough to hold the glass candleholder in place as well as support the weight of both the glass candleholder and the candle. You may want to size it a little snug and then wedge the candleholder in place when the glue is completely dry. Join the final pieces together and, when the glue has dried, insert the candleholder and candle.

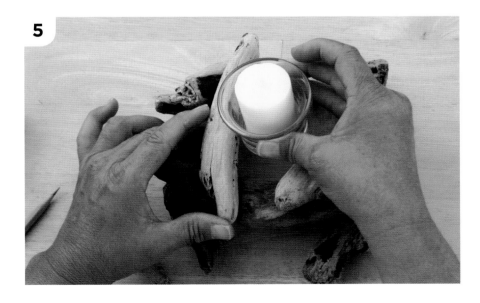

TIP
If you are nervous about applying the glue to the pieces of wood directly from the tube, use a cotton-tipped swab to apply it and have a damp paper towel handy to wipe off any excess.

Woodsy Opener

This bottle opener is sure to be a conversation piece at any party—just try not to brag too much about your crafting skills! You can mount the bottle opener to any secure, vertical surface where it will always be at hand.

MATERIALS

17–18 in. (43–45.7cm) piece of driftwood

Bottle opener

Two 1 in. (2.5cm) screws for bottle opener

Two 3 in. (7.6cm) anchor screws to secure the bottle opener to the wall

4 lengths of twine 6 in. (15cm) long (or 2 pieces each long enough to wrap around your piece of driftwood twice)

TOOLS

Table saw

Pencil

Drill

Piece of scrap wood or corkboard to use as a drilling base

Drill bit the same size as the 1 in. (2.5cm) screws

Drill bit slightly larger than the size of the 3 in. (7.6cm) screws

Screwdriver with same head as screws

Scissors

Wood glue

Woodsy Opener

1 Decide which side of the piece of driftwood will be the front. Use a table saw to shave the back of the piece of driftwood so it will rest flat against the wall.

2 Place the bottle opener in the desired position on the front of the driftwood and use a pencil to mark the position of each short screw. Drill shallow pilot holes (less than 1 in./2.5cm deep) into the wood. Secure the bottle opener to the driftwood using the 1 in. (2.5cm) screws.

3 Measure the point 2½ in. (6.3cm) from each end (the top and bottom) of the driftwood and drill a pilot hole using a drill bit slightly larger than the 3 in. (7.6cm) screws.

TIP
The holes drilled in the top and bottom of the driftwood will be used to secure the bottle opener to the wall using the long screws. Be sure the screws easily pass through the wood so that you can secure the bottle opener to the wall.

4 To mark the position of the twine accents, measure the points 2 in. (5cm) above and below the bottle opener and make a small pencil mark. Wrap the twine around the driftwood twice at this point and secure using wood glue. Let dry completely.

5 Decide the place on the wall where you want the bottle opener to hang. Holding the bottle opener in place, drill through the pilot holes in the driftwood and into the wall at the top of the opener, then insert one of the long screws and tighten. Repeat at the bottom of the opener.

TIP
The bottle opener needs to be secure since you'll be leveraging bottle tops against it to open them. Rather than drilling pilot holes into the wall first, it is best to screw it directly into the wall (or tree!).

Log

Sturdy and rustic, logs bring the spirit
of the woods into your home. From
the simple, a table made from a slice of
wood mounted on metal legs, to complex
assemblages of logs, boards, and branches,
there is a project to suit every skill level.
An elegant lamp base and a colorfully
upcycled planter round out the
offerings in this chapter.

Neat
Two-seater

You'll feel like a true woodsman building this rustic hall bench made completely from found logs and sturdy branches.

MATERIALS

4 pieces reclaimed wood for the cross braces, 12 in. (30.5cm) long x 1 in. (2.5cm) wide

4 pieces reclaimed wood for the legs, 18 in. (45.7cm) tall x 2½–3½ in. (6.3–9cm) wide

4 pieces reclaimed wood for length supports, 36 in. (91.5cm) long x 1 in. (2.5cm) wide

20–24 slats for the bench, 18 in. (45.7cm) long and of varying widths and textures

Sixteen 2½ in. (6.3cm) screws

Forty to forty-eight 1⅝ in. (4cm) #8 screws (2 for each slat)

TOOLS

Table saw

Miter saw

Drill with drill bit the same size as the screws, 1 in. (2.5cm) flare bit, and screwdriver bit

Measuring tape

Pencil

Neat Two-seater

1 Reduce the size of the ends of the wood selected for the cross braces by making a series of quick cuts so that they will fit the 1 in. (2.5cm) holes you will make with the flare bit.

2 Use the flare bit to make connecting holes at the end of each leg. Rotating the leg so that the holes are at a 90-degree angle, drill another hole 8 in. (20.3cm) below the first set of holes, to act as a second set of support holes. Repeat on all four legs.

3 Drill a pilot hole in each flare hole. (In each set, one pilot hole should angle downward and the other upward so that the screws don't collide.)

TIP
When working on the slats, sand down any rough edges on the wood and decide whether you want to countersink the screws so they sit flush with the surface of the bench (see page 118).

4 On one side of the bench, fit the cross brace pieces into the hole and then insert the 2½ in. (6.3cm) screws. Repeat for the other side. Prop both sides up and insert the length supports. Insert the screws. Repeat on the other side.

5 Lay the slat pieces across the top of the completed bench base. Drill a pilot hole in each end where the slat lies over the length supports. Repeat for each slat.

6 Insert a 1⅝ in. (4cm) screw through each pilot hole to secure a slat to the length support. Repeat for each slat.

Birch Log Bookshelf

This elegant shelving unit will add natural appeal to any wall in your home. Use it to display books, cherished items, and photos.

MATERIALS

Five shelves, cut to varying lengths 36–48 in. (91.5–122cm) and to widths of 5–8 in. (12.5–20.3cm); maple, poplar, and birch are all good choices

8–10 birch logs, cut in pairs of varying lengths between 8–12 in. (20.3–30.5cm) (some of the logs will be decorative and won't need a partner)

4 screw-on furniture legs in your desired color/texture (the type suitable for a couch or chair)

Sixteen to twenty $1\frac{5}{8}$ in. (4cm) #8 screws (two for each log you intend to use)

400 grit sandpaper

Wood plugs (optional)

L-shaped brackets

TOOLS

Hand sander

Miter saw

Measuring tape or ruler

Pencil

Drill with drill bits

Scrap wood

Rubber mallet

Strong multipurpose craft glue

Birch Log Bookshelf

1 Sand the top of each shelf to ensure a smooth surface. Select the piece you'd like to be the top of the bookshelf and set aside.

2 Measure the logs to check the lengths. You will need a pair of support logs for each shelf. The number of decorative logs of varying lengths you require will depend on your preference. In the example shown here, there are eight support logs and two decorative logs.

3 Cut the logs to the measurement desired.

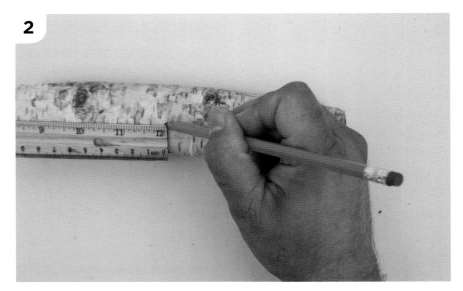

4 Work out the position of the logs. It doesn't necessarily matter how far in on each side the logs go, as long as they are centered on the width of the shelf. The example shown is 36 in. (91.5cm) long and 5½ in. (14cm) wide. For the shelf shown here, the log is centered 2¾ in. (7cm) on the width and 9 in. (22.8cm) from the long edge. Use a pencil to mark the position of the screws for the logs.

5 Lay a piece of scrap wood down on the work surface and place the shelf on top of it. Drill a pilot hole through the shelf on the two points marked in step 4.

6 Using a drill bit that is the same size as the head of the screw, drill a pilot hole the depth of the wood plug on both sides of the shelf.

7 Drill a shallow pilot hole into the two logs being used for this shelf.

Birch Log
Bookshelf

Before proceeding, decide which method of masking the screws you want to use. Option one is to use wood plugs to hide the screw heads. If you don't want to buy wood plugs, the other option is to save some of the sawdust from the project, add a dab of glue on top of each screw and sprinkle the sawdust into the hole. With both options, the important thing to remember is that you will have to countersink the screws (see Techniques, page 118).

8 Start to insert the screws through the pilot holes in the shelf by hand.

9 Holding the log against the screw, drill the screw through both the log and shelf to secure. Repeat for the other pilot hole.

10 Be sure to countersink the screws so they are below the surface of the shelf to leave room for the wood plug.

11 Depending on which option for masking the screws you have chosen (see box above), cover the screws. Wood plugs are shown here. Add a dab of glue to each screw head and place the wood plug into the hole.

12 Use a rubber mallet to gently tap the wood plug until it is flush with the shelf.

13 Next, attach the second shelf. Repeat steps 4 and 5 to measure where you want the logs to go and drill the pilot holes. Attach the shelf following the instructions in steps 6–12. Repeat the process until the desired number of shelves is complete.

14 When you have the desired number of shelves, add the furniture legs. There will be two legs on each side. Make sure they are evenly spaced. Using a drill bit slightly thinner than the leg screw, drill a pilot hole around the same length as the screw.

15 Insert the furniture legs. Repeat the process on the other side.

SAFETY

For extra security, be sure to secure the bookshelf to the wall with a couple of small L-shaped brackets.

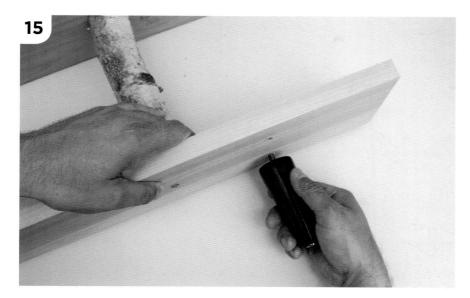

Chunky Table

Add a touch of mid-century glamour to your yard or living room by creating this simple end table. Look for a section of log with an attractive shape and interesting markings for a piece of furniture that will be as useful as it is eye-catching.

MATERIALS

Cut log for tabletop, the one shown measures 14 x 11 in. (35.5 x 28cm) and is 3¼ in. (8.2cm) thick

3–4 metal hairpin table legs, 16 in. (40.5cm) tall and with clip-on floor protectors (available online)

Sixteen 1¼ in. (3.1cm) size 8 screws

TOOLS

Hand sander

Drill

TIP
If you use a freshly cut— also known as a "green" — log your tabletop will have a bright surface. If you use dried wood it will be darker.

1 Decide which side of the log will be the top of the table and use a hand sander to sand it smooth.

2 Place the sanded side of the tabletop facedown on a clean work surface. Arrange the legs in the desired configuration and secure with the screws. Clip on the floor protectors.

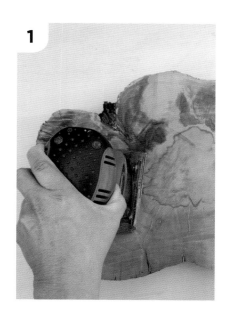

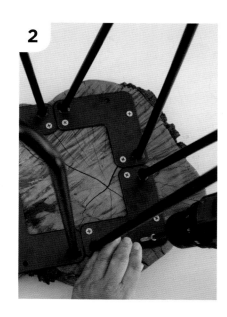

Vibrant Vertical Planter

Whether in your garden or among potted plants on your balcony, this playfully rustic planter is sure to brighten anyone's day! Choose cans large enough to hold your favorite flowering plants, or perhaps you prefer cascades of tomatoes, herbs, or strawberries.

MATERIALS

3 cans

Acrylic, waterproof paint in 1 to 3 colors

4 pieces of scrap pallet wood each 8–10 in. (20.3–25.4cm) long

8 screws—we used 1⅝ in. (4cm) Phillips-head screws, but any 2 in. (5cm) gray screw will work well

Log, 36–48 in. (91.5–122cm) long and 4 in. (10cm) in diameter

TOOLS

Paintbrushes or sponges

Table saw, or a similar setup

Drill with Phillips-head drill bit and drill bit for pilot holes (1/32 size works well for these screws)

Vibrant Vertical Planter

1 Paint your cans and let them dry (see Tip, below).

2 While the painted cans are drying, use the scrap pallet wood to make a base. Cut all four pieces the same length (about 8–10 in./20.3–25.4cm) and create a pinwheel-shaped base with a central opening large enough to hold the log securely. Size it so that it's snug enough to hold the log on its own, but not so tight that you won't be able to tighten it if needed.

TIP
We roughly dabbed the paint on using a sponge for a more weathered look, but you can also use a paintbrush or sponge with broader strokes, and apply multiple coats for full coverage.

3 Holding two of the base pieces together, drill a pilot hole where the pieces of wood have the strongest connection (see page 118). Then, drill the screws in to secure the base pieces together. Repeat until all pieces are secured.

4 Insert the log into the completed base. Holding it in place, drill pilot holes on each side of the base, then insert the screws into each hole and tighten them to secure it.

5 When your log has been secured into the base on all sides, it's time to add the cans. Decide which side you want to be the front of the first can, and drill a pilot hole through the metal on the opposite side, which will be the back. Decide where you will position the can on the log and attach it with a screw. You can create another pilot hole or just drill straight into the wood. Repeat with the remaining cans.

Log-stack Lamp

Brighten the corner of a room and get that expensive handcrafted look at a fraction of the cost. Plus you'll have the satisfaction of making it with your own hands! This lamp base is formed from disks of wood stacked on top of each other.

MATERIALS

Log, 3–4 in. (7.6–10cm) in diameter and 14 in. (35.5cm) long

Lamp kit

Lamp harp or UNO lampshade adapter

Wood glue

Lampshade

TOOLS

Miter saw

Ruler

Pencil

Drill with drill bit the same size as the lamp cord

Piece of scrap wood or corkboard to use as a drilling base

Needle-nosed pliers

Log-stack Lamp

1 Mark 1 in. (2.5cm) spaces along the log. Use the miter saw to cut the log into fourteen pieces 1 in. (2.5cm) thick.

2 Find the center of the pieces of wood by measuring them vertically and horizontally and marking the point where the lines intersect. Using a piece of scrap wood or corkboard as a drilling base, drill a hole through the center of each one.

3 Select the piece of wood that will form the base of the lamp and drill a second hole horizontally through the center of one side; this hole should connect with the existing central hole but should not extend beyond the hole. It will form a channel for the cord.

4 Thread the lamp cord through the base, starting with the horizontal hole. Then thread it through the remaining pieces of wood. If necessary, use a pencil to push it into the holes, and needle-nosed pliers to pull it through.

5 Following the package instructions, fit the lamp kit to the top of the pieces of wood. Position the base of the lamp socket in the drilled hole. Secure the wiring using an underwriter's knot (see page 121). Connect the wiring into the main socket by loosening the screw, hooking the end of the wire around the terminal, and tightening the screw. Repeat this on the other terminal.

6 Push the socket together so that the wiring is on the inside. Secure with a screw.

7 Secure the socket to the base following the package instructions.

8 Working downward from the top of the lamp, use wood glue to secure each piece of wood to the next until you reach the base. Let dry completely.

9 Add the lamp harp or shade adapter to hold the shade and the bulb.

TIP

Silver birch logs make an elegant white lamp base. You can buy pre-cut birch disks online.

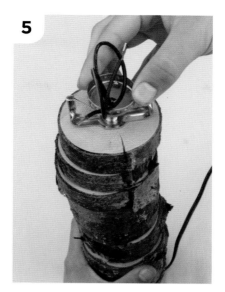

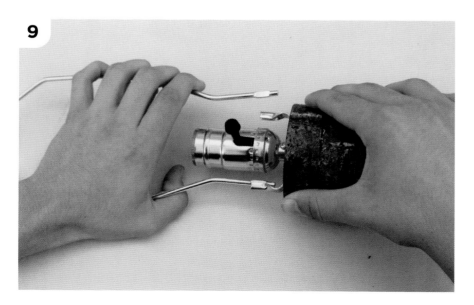

Board

Whether you have a short piece of board or a whole pallet, this chapter shows you how to make something beautiful out of it. Using boards, you can make a sign, build a shelf or a bathtub tray, put together a planter, or create a clock. Let the wood speak for itself or embellish your creations with stencils to provide the perfect finishing touch.

Beach This Way!

Whether you want to point the way to the beach, your yard, or your kitchen, this sign will show guests the way.

MATERIALS

Piece of board about 4 x 8 in. (10 x 20.3cm)

Two small nails or tacks

Length of twine, 14–16 in. (35.5–40.5cm)

Glue (optional)

White paint

TOOLS

Hammer

Foam paintbrush

Stencil saying "beach" with an arrow, sized about 2¼ x 6 in. (5.7 x 15.2cm) (see page 122)

Repositionable spray adhesive or low-tack masking tape

TIP
You can spell out any word or message you like. Just remember to choose a piece of board long enough to hold all the letters you need.

Beach This Way!

1 Holding the piece of board horizontally, attach a nail at each side edge, positioning them ½ in. (1.3cm) down from the top edge.

2 Secure the ends of the twine around each nail using a simple knot. You can add a dab of glue to secure the knots if you wish.

3 Place your stencil in the desired position on the piece of wood and secure in place using repositionable spray adhesive or low-tack masking tape.

4 Lightly dab paint onto the stencil to fill in the letters, being careful not to put too much paint under the edges of the letters. Carefully remove the stencil and let dry.

STENCILING METHODS

Stenciling is easy when you know how. You can either use a ready-made template (see pages 122–125) or create your own stencil. Once you have mastered the art of stenciling, you can add a touch of whimsy and fun to your wood projects.

MAKING A CUSTOM STENCIL

To create a bespoke stencil, photocopy or trace the letters you need onto a sheet of paper and cut them out. The method below guarantees that your letters will be straight and evenly spaced.

- Use a ruler and pen or pencil to draw a straight line onto a piece of thin cardboard or sheet of plastic. Copy or trace the letters onto the cardboard or plastic using the line as a guide to ensure that they are straight.

- When you are happy with the placement of the letters, use a sharp pair of scissors to cut out each one, making sure the edges are neat. You will apply the paint through the holes you have created.

- Alternatively, type your letters into a word processing program and print them out, scaling them up or down so that they fit your piece of wood. Copy or trace the letters and then cut them out as before.

- Once your stencil is ready, position it over your piece of wood and secure in place with repositionable spray glue or low-tack masking tape.

- Dip the tip of your paintbrush into the paint and dab off the excess onto a piece of scrap paper—it's better to build up several thin layers of paint until you have the coverage you want, than try to remove excess paint if you use too much.

- Carefully remove the stencil while the paint is wet (this prevents the dry paint from "gluing" the stencil to the wood and spoiling the finish when you try to remove it) and let dry.

DIE-CUT STENCILS

You can buy these from your local craft store or online. Alternatively, if you have a die-cutting machine designed for scrapbooking, you can use it to create your own stencil.

PERFECT RESULTS

To achieve professional-looking results, hold the brush perpendicular to the wood and carefully dab the paint onto the stencil to fill in the letters, making sure it covers the edges so that each letter is filled in.

Garden Planter

Show off your green thumb and your carpentry skills with this easy upcycled planter. Use reclaimed wood in different widths and painted in several colors to ensure there is plenty of visual interest.

MATERIALS

Piece of ¾ in. (2cm) plywood, 12 in. (30.5cm) square

Reclaimed painted pieces of wood, 12 in. (30.5cm) tall. You will need enough pieces to measure about 48 in. (122cm) wide in total when placed side by side

Four pieces reclaimed wood, 15 in. (38cm) long

Four pieces wood, cut into isosceles triangles and with the equal sides both 2½ in. (6.3cm) long

Thirty-two to thirty-six 1⅝ in. (4cm) #8 screws

TOOLS

Table saw

Miter saw

Drill with drill bit the same size as the screws and drill bit desired size for drainage holes

Screwdriver bit

Measuring tape

Pencil

Garden Planter

1 Place the plywood square on a flat surface. Join the pieces of reclaimed wood to the edges of the square and at right-angles to it to create the sides of the planter. To do this, drill pilot holes through each side piece and into the base. Secure with screws. Repeat until all the pieces of reclaimed wood are secured around the base.

2 To secure the top corner at each side, drill a pilot hole through the section where the sides join 1 in. (2.5cm) from top and then secure with a screw.

3 To make the top of the sides, miter the ends of the 15 in. (38cm) long pieces of reclaimed wood. Turn the miter saw to a 45-degree angle and cut both ends of each piece of wood so that the shorter, inside edge of the mitered wood measures 12 in. (30.5cm) long.

4 Arrange the pieces of mitered wood on the top of the sides of the planter so that the inside edge is flush with the side piece and the ridge hangs slightly over the outside of the planter. Drill two pilot holes and then secure with screws.

5 Drill three large holes into the base for drainage.

6 With the bottom of the planter facing up, secure a wood triangle at each corner to act as feet. Drill pilot holes and then secure with screws.

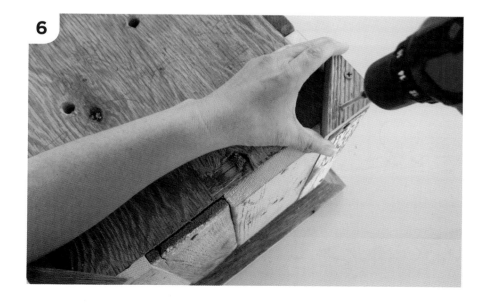

Bathtub Tray

This handy tray will hold everything you need for a relaxing soak in the tub and it takes less than 60 minutes to make! Because it will get wet, use a mold and mildew resistant waterproof sealant.

MATERIALS

4 pieces of reclaimed wood, 30 in. (76cm) long

2 pieces reclaimed wood, 14 in. (35.5cm) long

Urethane waterproof sealant

Eight ¾ in. (2cm) screws

TOOLS

Sandpaper

Brush

Carpenter's square (square ruler)

Clamp

Drill with drill bit the same size as the screws

Piece of scrap cardboard

Paintbrush to apply sealant

Bathtub Tray

1 Sand the edges of each piece of wood, then brush off any excess dust or debris.

2 Assemble the tray upside down. Place the four long planks side by side and use the carpenter's square to make sure the edges are correctly aligned.

3 Use the clamp to secure the planks together so they are tightly held in place. Use the carpenter's square to make sure each corner forms a right angle.

TIP

The four longer wood planks should be long enough to allow for 3 in. (7.6cm) of wood to overhang both sides of the bathtub. The two smaller pieces are positioned to fit the interior width of the tub to keep the tray in place while it's being used. Measure the width of your tub to check that the measurements given here are long enough, and either cut the planks to fit, or find longer planks if they are too short.

1

2

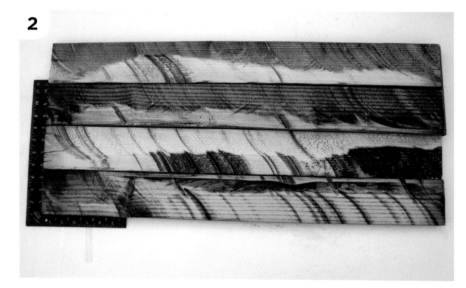

3

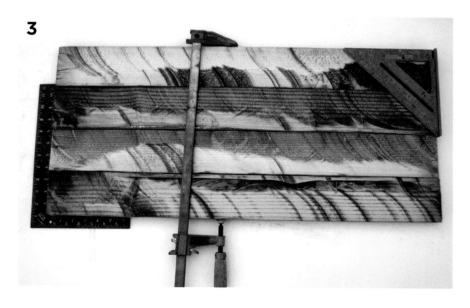

4 Position the two shorter pieces of wood on each side of the tray, running across the long planks. Remember to place them so that they will sit inside your bathtub widthwise. Drill very shallow pilot holes in the two short pieces of wood—they should only be deep enough to break through the first layer of wood.

5 Drill all the screws into the pilot holes, being careful to ensure all four pieces are held together tightly and the bottom small pieces are flush with the top tray pieces.

6 Brush off the excess dust and debris from all the surfaces of the tray. Protecting the work surface with scrap cardboard, paint the wood with sealant. Start on the underside, focusing on the edges, ends, and gaps between the pieces of wood. Let dry completely before flipping over and painting the top of the tray.

TIP
Be sure to use screws that are long enough to connect the two pieces of wood but do not breach the top of the tray.

Easy Pallet Shelving

This piece is a great example of creative upcycling! Turn a pallet into a beautiful rustic statement piece that's the perfect place to store a favorite book or display treasured keepsakes. You only need a section of the pallet—or more of it to make a set of matching shelves.

MATERIALS

Pallet

Six 1⅝ in. (4cm) #8 screws

Wood stain

Hanger that will hold the weight of the shelf

TOOLS

Ruler

Pencil

Circular saw

Hammer

Drill with drill bit to fit existing holes in the wood

Screwdriver bit

Hand sander with 60 or 80 grit sandpaper

Scrap cardboard or newspaper

Latex gloves

Rag

Scrap cardboard or newspaper

Easy Pallet Shelving

1 The shelf consists of a 14 in. (35.5cm) deep section of the pallet with two pieces of the top deck board and the supports, plus an additional plank that serves as the backing. To separate the main section from the pallet, use a ruler and pencil to measure and mark a line on each runner 14 in. (35.5cm) from one long edge of the pallet. Use a circular saw to cut along the lines on each side of the pallet.

2 To cut through the middle section of the pallet, lay the pallet down on the ground and cut from the top to remove the 14 in. (35.5cm) deep section of the pallet.

3 Pry one board from the remaining pallet by hammering the back (reverse end) of the nails to loosen them. Then use the claw of the hammer to remove the board. Discard the nails and the rest of the pallet.

4 Place the 14 in. (35.5cm) section of pallet on the ground so that the top deck board timbers are on the bottom. Place the single board across the section of pallet to create the shelf backing. Secure in place by inserting screws through the holes left by the nails.

5 Use the hand sander to sand all the surfaces of the wood to smooth them and remove any splinters but be careful to keep the rustic appearance.

6 Using scrap cardboard or newspaper to protect the work surface and gloves to protect your hands, use a rag to apply a generous amount of wood stain to the shelf. Let dry.

7 Attach the hanger to the back of the frame. Drill pilot holes into the frame and then secure the hanger with screws.

TIP
Look for a hanger designed for paintings or heavy photo frames with a 25-pound rating. You can use a single hanger in the center of the shelf, or put one on each side of the back to make it even more secure. This is essential if you plan to put heavy items on the shelf.

Timber Timepiece

As well as always knowing the time, you'll have a sense of accomplishment every time you look up at this clock. The reclaimed wood face conceals a battery-operated clock mechanism; similar kits are available from craft stores or online—choose one that suits your decor.

MATERIALS

5 pieces of reclaimed wood, 14½ in. (36.6cm) long, about 3 in. (7.6cm) wide

2 pieces of wood, 12 in. (30.5cm) long, ½ in. (1.3cm) thick

Clock kit

Ten ¾ in. (2cm) screws

TOOLS

Drill

Drill bit the same size as screws

Drill bit the same size as clock hardware

13–in. (33cm) diameter plate or similar item to use as a template

Pencil

Jigsaw

Hand sander

Timber Timepiece

1 Place the five pieces of reclaimed wood on a flat surface so that they are aligned and facedown. Place one of the support pieces at each end of the reclaimed wood slats so that they are at right angles to them and about 3 in. (7.6cm) from the ends. Drill five pilot holes into each support piece to join each piece of reclaimed wood to both supports. Be sure not to drill through to the clockface. Insert the screws to secure the clockface to the supports.

2 Turn the joined wood over. Using a pencil and a large plate or similar item as a template, draw a 13 in. (33cm) circle onto the wood for the clockface. Cut along the marked line using the jigsaw.

3 Use a hand sander to smooth the cut edges of the wood.

4 Find the center of the clockface by measuring it vertically and horizontally and marking the point where the lines intersect. Drill a hole the same size as the clock kit hardware at the center point.

5 Insert the clock mechanism through the hole and screw it in place until it is snug. Following the package instructions, attach the clock kit base washer, small locking nut, hour hand, minute hand, locking nut, and second hand.

TIP
The two pieces of wood measuring 12 in. (30.5cm) long are used to support the clockface. They must be thick enough to hold the clock kit and allow the finished clock to sit flush against the wall. For the kit used here, the wood was ½ in. (1.3cm) thick, but check your kit before choosing your wood.

Techniques

Some of the techniques used for working with found wood are the same as for any other type of wood. This section tells you what tools you'll need and how to use them, as well as showing you how to tie some handy knots. The real joy of working with found wood is in the finding. We tell you where to look and what to look out for!

Choosing and Using Found Wood

Driftwood

Bleached and beautiful, smoothed and silky, driftwood is one of my favorite materials. It lives up to its name, having spent time in the water drifting, floating, and being tumbled by river currents or ocean waves, and sometimes both! The wood may be deposited on a riverbank or ocean beach to bleach and dry out only to be picked up and carried on another journey by high tides or river flows. If only the wood could tell us about its journey! Driftwood may originate from high in the mountain forests, it might have been part of a boat that was lost at sea, or it could be an ocean pier that succumbed to the power of the currents. Coming in all shapes and sizes, driftwood looks great when it has been tossed by the water and aged and bleached by the sun. Its naturally rounded edges and soft gray-white colors give it an ageless appeal.

Choosing and Using Found Wood

WHERE TO LOOK

Since the wood is shaped by water through the tumbling action of surf or the swirl of a swiftly moving current, beaches are the best places to find driftwood. But not just any beach or shore will yield treasure. The best places to find driftwood are within a mile or two of the mouth of a river or on a beach that has strong currents. You are less likely to find it in a tranquil bay.

Look for a naturally flowing river that hasn't been dammed and that has a year-round rather than a seasonal flow. Wood carried by wild and natural rivers comes from fallen trees and branches.

Avoid rivers that are surrounded by housing developments or urban sprawl, as they do not yield much driftwood. When people live near rivers, they tend to want to control and tame the water for their own benefit, so losing the natural strength of the water that washes wood downstream.

The beaches of northern California, Oregon, and Washington state are incredible places to find driftwood, from small pieces that fit in your pocket to giant tree trunks and huge branches that can take two or more people to carry. They are brought to the Pacific Ocean by fast-flowing rivers with thick forests growing right to the water's edge. The ocean currents are very strong and many beaches are littered with naturally aged and tumbled driftwood. This is my happy hunting ground. Even if you don't live near the ocean, you should be able to find a river or lake that will reward you with great driftwood finds.

WHAT TO LOOK FOR

When choosing driftwood, it really comes down to what you like and what's available. If there is an abundance of wood, you can afford to be more selective. At other times, make do with what you find. We love wood that has been naturally worn and "sanded" by the elements and bleached by the sun. If there is a lot of wood on a beach, look above the high-tide line. This is where you'll find the wood that has been on the beach longest, perhaps deposited by a storm surge or a super-high tide and left to bleach and age. That doesn't mean there aren't great pieces along the waterline though! Take your time: The search for the right piece of driftwood is as much fun as the joy when you find it.

PREPARING THE DRIFTWOOD

I don't do much to the wood besides thoroughly drying it and then brushing any loose sand or debris off the surface with a soft brush. However, some people soak the wood in fresh water to remove any saltwater. Be careful not to brush or clean too much because you risk losing the patina that nature provided, and you may scratch the wood if it's soft or wet.

For small pieces of driftwood, soaking in bleach and water lightens the wood and kills any critters. Make a soaking mixture using 2 cups (500ml) of bleach to a gallon (4.5l) of water. Put your driftwood pieces in a bucket and add enough of the bleach mixture to cover. If the pieces float, use a flat rock to keep them submerged. Leave for five days, changing the bleach water daily. Drain and allow them to dry naturally.

Logs

Look for logs in hard-to-reach places, perhaps where they have been embedded between large rocks or boulders on a riverbank edge or on the edge of a forest. You can also buy logs (see page 126). Bought logs will have been heat-treated and so have the advantage of being bug free. If you know anyone who has had to cut down a tree, ask them for a log or two.

Use hardwood such as ash, birch, beech, cherry, elm, hickory, maple, or oak rather than softwood such as pine or spruce. The log should feel heavy. Choose solid pieces that are free of decay. To check that the wood is suitable, bang it against a rock—if there's a dull thud, it's rotten. Don't bother with it!

Use a soft brush to clean off dirt and debris, then spray with insecticide (see box). If there's any rot, cut around it.

COMMON HARDWOOD TREES IN NORTH AMERICA

- ash: genus *Fraxinus*
- beech: genus *Fagus*
- basswood: genus *Tilia*
- birchwood: genus *Betula*
- black cherry: genus *Prunus*
- black walnut/butternut: genus *Juglans*
- cottonwood: genus *Populus*
- elm: genus *Ulmus*
- hackberry: genus *Celtis*
- hickory: genus *Carya*
- holly: genus *Ilex*
- locust: genus *Robinia* and *Gleditsia*
- magnolia: genus *Magnolia*
- maple: genus *Acer*
- oak: genus *Quercus*
- poplar: genus *Populus*
- red alder: genus *Alnus*
- royal paulownia: genus *Paulownia*
- sassafras: genus *Sassafras*
- sweetgum: genus *Liquidambar*
- sycamore: genus *Platanus*
- tupelo: genus *Nyssa*
- willow: genus *Salix*
- yellow poplar: genus *Liriodendron*

MAKE IT PEST FREE

Found wood might have been someone else's home before you moved it into your own! To avoid bringing any creepy-crawlies inside, you will need to treat the wood with an insecticide. Mix insecticide with water in a spray bottle. Take the wood you are treating outside and place it on newspaper or cardboard to avoid getting the insecticide on any surfaces. Spray each piece thoroughly with the insecticide mixture. Leave to dry naturally—large pieces may take a few days to dry completely.

Twigs and Branches

You can find fallen twigs and branches in your own backyard or in public woodlands. Be sure to take only fallen twigs or branches; do not cut them from living trees (unless they belong to you, of course). Be careful to avoid trespassing on private property.

Look for interesting shapes or colors. I always keep an eye out for branches from less common trees and for gnarled roots with character. Pick up wood that is the right size for the project you are planning. Even small twigs can be used, as in the Twig Vase (see page 10), while a group of branches can add interest to your hallway as a Rustic Coatrack (see page 32).

I find that Mother Nature has usually taken care of most of the cleaning, so just spot clean with a brush as necessary. However, if your finds are muddy or dirty, you will need to rinse them in water and scrub with a wire brush. If the mud is dry, let the wood soak until any dirt is soft enough to come off easily. You do not want to scrub so hard that you remove the bark. Allow the wood to dry naturally in a well-ventilated room.

Boards

Old boards can be found almost everywhere; you might even have some in your garage. When you are out looking for driftwood, you may come across sea-weathered boards. You can also break up old pallets and crates; look for them at yard sales.

If you want a weathered look, seek out wood that has been exposed to the elements, such as driftwood, weathered crates or pallets, collapsed barns or sheds, or old doors.

Be sure not to trespass and don't take anything without asking the property owner for permission.

Old boards may have nails. Remove these first. Then use a brush to clean off dirt and debris. Boards have often been painted. I love the look of weathered paint and only remove loose or flaking paint. Be sure to wear a mask and dispose of the flakes appropriately as the paint may contain lead.

As with all found wood, insects may be present, so the wood will need to be treated (see page 111) before you bring it indoors.

STAY LEGAL

Unless you are on your own property or on that of someone who has given you permission to gather wood, you will need to obey any local, state, or federal laws governing collecting wood. It is your responsibility to find out what they are as ignorance is not a defense!

GATHERING DRIFTWOOD

All of our driftwood is from the California coast where I live. Here the official limit for taking driftwood is 50 lbs (23kg) per person, per day, as long as the wood is taken from above the high-tide line and there are no living organisms in it. Be sure to check that there are no hermit crabs using the wood for a home. Look out, too, for nesting birds and other living creatures. "Taken above the high-tide line" means above the point reached by the water during high tide: Look for the place where the sand stops being wet. Each state and every country has its own rules for collecting driftwood; be sure to check local regulations. You can also buy driftwood online (see page 126).

GATHERING WOOD

You are unlikely to get into trouble for picking up the few fallen twigs needed to make the Twig Vase (see page 10), but taking more wood or large logs and branches may be another matter. On land owned by the U.S. Department of the Interior, you are allowed to take reasonable amounts for personal use without a permit—for example, enough to make a fire. State and local parks may have different rules, so check before you remove any wood.

DON'T SPREAD DISEASE

In recent years, the risk of spreading infestations of insects by moving firewood long distances has become better known. The USDA has asked people not to transport firewood as it may be harboring invasive insect pests. Thirty states have restrictions on transporting wood, largely in response to the problems caused by the emerald ash borer. When gathering wood for your projects, it's best to find it within 10 miles (16km) of where you live. Wood that has been kiln dried at a temperature of 160°F (70°C) for at least 75 minutes is safe. If buying online, be sure that you are buying kiln-dried wood.

Tools and Equipment

THE ESSENTIALS

- Sandpaper (100–180 grit), glue, screws and/or nails, screwdrivers (Phillips-head and flat-head), carpenter's square, hammer, handsaw, wood file, paintbrushes, clamps

ADVANCED ITEMS

- Power drill, miter saw, table saw, palm sander, planer, circular saw

SAFETY EQUIPMENT

- plastic/rubber gloves
- goggles or protective eyeglasses
- dust mask

HOW TO CARE FOR YOUR TOOLS

- Store indoors away from the elements, clean on a regular basis, lubricate moving parts as per manufacturer instructions, change blades as needed.

HAND TOOLS VS. POWER TOOLS

- Hand tools can be essential when adding finishing touches to a piece. Sanding by hand, adding a screw in a small space, or adding a protective finish are often things that can only be done by hand. Power tools, however, are essential for cutting wood to save time and energy.

SAFETY

Always wear a mask and eye protection while working with wood, paints, stains, and other finishes, and be sure to follow any safety advice on labels. Do not use power tools without proper training.

HAND PLANERS

A planer is great for leveling surfaces. The Trio of Coat Hooks (see page 24) uses the planer to give a flat surface for mounting on the wall. However, a planer is not a tool that you will use on every project, so it's a luxury rather than a must-have. When using a planer, be sure to place both hands in the correct position for equal pressure. Don't press down hard on the surface being leveled—let the tool do the work. Start on one end of the surface to be planed and move slowly and methodically to the other end. Be consistent in moving in one direction. As with sanding, go "with the grain," following the direction of the long grain.

TOOL	WHAT IS IT USED FOR?	WHY IS IT WORTH HAVING IN YOUR TOOL BOX?
Table saw	straight cuts on large wood	essential for big cuts
Miter saw	angle and end cuts	for angle cuts
Circular saw	fast straight-line cutting	versatile and mobile
Planer	leveling uneven surfaces	for a professional finish
Drill with drill bits	making solid joints and connecting pieces of wood with screws and bolts	to save time and effort
Palm sander	finishing work, leveling work	for a professional finish
Tape measure	measuring	for accuracy
Phillips-head screwdriver	screwing in Phillips-head screws	Phillips-head screws are the most common type
Scissors	cutting rope	essential
Paintbrushes	applying finishes	essential
Clamps	holding pieces of wood together while wood glue is setting	for secure bonds

Measuring and Sawing

MEASURING TECHNIQUES

As the old saying goes, measure twice, cut once! In other words, avoid errors by checking your measurements two or three times before cutting your materials. When measuring for a cut, remember that the cut should be made on the outside of the measurement (on the side you won't be using). If you cut right on the line, the blade of the saw will reduce the measurement, making it shorter than you require.

A thumb lock on the front of the tape measure allows you to lock the tape measure to a certain length. Always mark your measurements in pencil so that you can erase any stray marks once a job is complete.

A speed carpenter's square is a great tool. Use it to measure corners and right angles quickly and accurately. It typically has a lipped edge that can be pressed against the flat side of a piece of wood to ensure greater accuracy.

 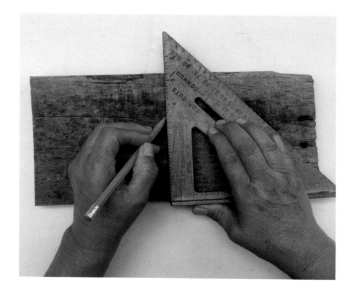

SAWING TECHNIQUES

Always wear protective eyewear when using power tools. You don't want anything getting caught in the machinery, so don't wear loose scarves, jewelry, gloves, or belts.

When using a handsaw, make sure your support hand is clear of the cutting line and the movement of the blade. And go slow, keeping the blade on the line. The cutting action is the downward stroke, when you put pressure on the saw and the wood. The upward stroke brings the saw back into the cutting position.

When using a table saw or circular saw, remember that the blade is moving at high speed and can catch and cause injury if you try to force it through the wood. Be patient and let the sawblade do its job. Forcing a circular saw through hardwood or forcing hardwood through a table saw can cause inaccurate cuts and possible injury.

Joining and Drilling

JOINING TECHNIQUES

When joining pieces of driftwood together, you are rarely going to have flat pieces that can be easily glued (see page 119), which means you sometimes have to be creative. If you can't use a clamp to apply pressure when gluing uneven driftwood pieces, try a heavy object like a brick or stone to apply pressure. If that doesn't work, use duct tape. You can carefully remove the tape once the glue is dry. Your aim is to apply pressure to ensure the best bond possible.

When you have flat pieces with a large contact point, use a clamp. Wood clamps come in a variety of sizes for all kinds of projects, big or small.

When joining pieces with a screw, hold or clamp the pieces together and then drill a pilot hole using a bit smaller than the size of screw (see below). Insert the screw into the pilot hole while the wood is still clamped and then remove the clamps.

DRILLING TECHNIQUES

When joining pieces of wood together with a screw, it is always best to drill a pilot hole first. This is a small hole that you drill as a guide to where you will drill the larger hole for your screw. A pilot hole will make sure the screw is going where you intend it to go, and it will help prevent the wood from splitting. If you just drill a screw into wood without a pilot hole, the wood will crack and separate. When drilling a pilot hole, make sure the drill bit is smaller than the diameter of the screw. If the bit is too big, the screw won't get a tight grip inside the wood and your joint will not be secure. Likewise, if the drill bit is too small, the screw may become difficult to insert or the wood might split. Before drilling, press the bit against the wood and look at the angle of your drill from the top and the sides before you drill. You can also use a square to ensure good technique.

For a neat finish, countersink your screws. Countersinking a hole is basically creating a "crater" for the screw head so that it sits flush with the surface. After you have drilled a pilot hole, use a larger drill bit (equal to the diameter of the screw head) and gently drill the top of the pilot hole with the larger bit but only drill down about $\frac{1}{16}$ in. (1.5mm)—just enough for the head of the screw to sit in the hole and be flush with the surface. When you are done, you should be able to slide a glass of water across the surface of the screw hole without a bump or interruption! Countersinking screws is really only important on the surface of a project. It is not necessary on the undersides or support areas of a project.

Finishing and Gluing

FINISHING TECHNIQUES

Prepare wood for finishing by sanding with 400 grit sandpaper. Try to sand "with the grain," meaning sand in the direction of the grain in the wood.

The optimum temperature for applying a finish is 55°–80°F (13°–26.5°C). When applying a finish outdoors, do so on a day with little or no wind. Dust and debris can stick to a finish while it is drying. When applying a finish indoors, make sure there is proper ventilation.

Any finish you apply, whether it's paint, varnish, polyurethane, or beeswax, seals the wood. All these finishes can be applied with a paintbrush, or fine steel wool in the case of beeswax. Don't stint on quality: the better the brush, the smoother the finish. Most finishes need two coats. If you like the natural look of the wood, but want something hard-wearing, use varnish or polyurethane. Varnish is an all-weather finish for outdoor use and polyurethane is an indoor finish.

Left to right: paint, polyurethane, beeswax

USING GLUE

When gluing wood, it's important to clean the surface as well as you can. You may need to use a coarse wire brush to brush off any debris. If you are working with a soft wood, use a gentler brush, similar to the one you might use for washing dishes. An old toothbrush is a great tool for cleaning small pieces of wood or getting into nooks and crannies.

Once the surface is free of as much debris as possible, decide how much glue you need. Are you repairing a split piece of wood? If so, you'll want to use a generous amount of wood glue and then clamp the piece tight until it dries, wiping off any excess. Are you securing a single shell to a piece of wood? Then you'll want to use a multipurpose glue to dab into the small space, or a Q-tip, and with a rag on hand for any excess.

Choosing the right glue really depends on what your goals are. If you're repairing wood, or doing something that's not crucial to the structural integrity of the project, wood glue is fine. If you want a more secure hold, you'll need to use a stronger multipurpose glue, such as E6000.

Knots

TYING A SIMPLE KNOT

For simple projects, sometimes all it takes is a simple knot! To tie such a knot, make a loop and insert one end of the string into the loop, then pull both ends in opposite directions.

MAKING A DOUBLE KNOT

Sometimes a sturdier knot is called for, and in that case you may want to use a double knot—like the simple knot, but with another loop! To tie a double knot, make a loop and insert one end of the string into the loop (steps 1 and 2). Before pulling both ends taut, insert the same end of the string into the loop again (3). Now gently pull both ends of the string taut (4) to create the double knot (5).

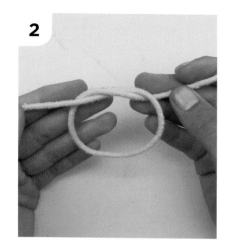

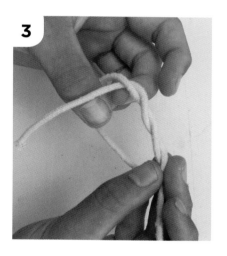

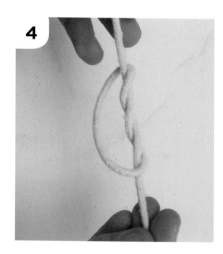

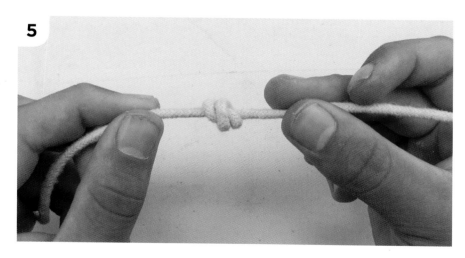

TYING AN UNDER-WRITER'S KNOT

For projects involving electrical wiring, an underwriter's knot is best. To make such a knot, first separate the two wires. (We have used string to show how to tie this knot.) Place the two wires parallel to each other (1). Form a loop with the first wire so that the bended end passes behind the cord (2), then make a loop with the other wire so that the bended end passes in front of the cord (3). You should now have two loops, one with the end passing around the back and one passing in front. Feed the loose end of each wire through the loop of the opposite wire (4) and pull the two ends in opposite directions (5)!

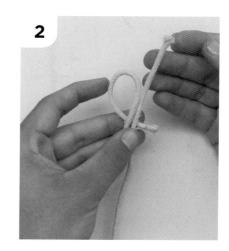

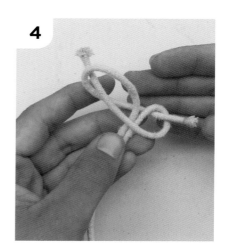

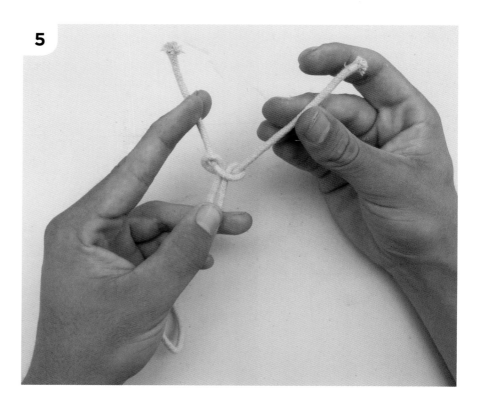

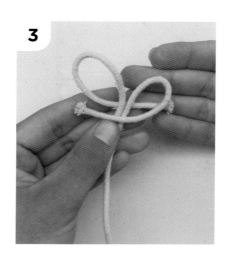

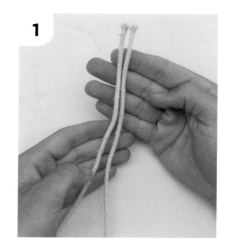

Templates

The Beach This Way! sign (see page 86) is the only stenciled project in this book, but stenciling can add interest to many other wooden projects. It's easiest on a flat surface so the projects in the board chapter will work best. For example, you could stencil numbers on to the Timber Timepiece on page 102 or embellish the Vibrant Vertical Planter (see page 76) with a row of sun symbols.

Once you've made your first stenciled sign, you are bound to want to make more. For a wedding gift, stencil the happy couple's names onto a board; for a house-warming present, the word "home" is simple and elegant. With more time (and a bigger board), you can stencil quotes and phrases that make beautiful additions to your home and meaningful gifts for friends and relatives.

Full directions on how to stencil can be found on page 89. Follow them and unleash your creativity.

abcdef
ghijklm
nopqrst
uvwxyz

ABCDEFG
HIJKLMN
OPQRST
UVWXYZ

01234 →
56789 ! ?

Resources

PAINT AND BRUSHES

Michael's: www.michaels.com
JOANN Fabrics and Crafts: www.joann.com

WOOD AND TOOLS

Home Depot: www.homedepot.com
Lowe's: www.lowes.com
Target: www.target.com

LOGS, BRANCHES, AND DRIFTWOOD

Etsy: www.etsy.com
Hobby Lobby: www.hobbylobby.com

HARDWARE AND MISCELLANEOUS SUPPLIES

eBay: www.ebay.com
Amazon: www.amazon.com
Ace Hardware: www.acehardware.com

SHELLS

Quality Shells: www.qualityshells.com
California Seashell Company: www.caseashells.com

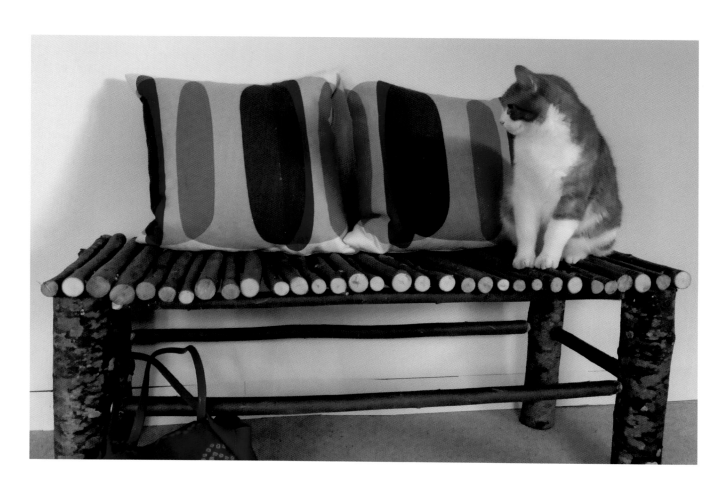

Index

Acknowledgments

Linda Suster would like to thank
Mike Suster, Megan Suster, Jack Suster, Emma Suster,
Abby Suster, Calvin Suster, and Steve Moreno-Terrill.

Toucan Books would like to thank
Penelope Armitage, Charlotte Cox, Dave Ham,
and Antonia and Peter van der Meer.

Picture Credits

All images by Linda Suster except as follows:
L=left, C = center, R=right

3 Claire Richardson/Narratives; 7 johnandersonphoto/iStock;
8-9 gerenme/iStock; 11 Dorling Kindersley Ltd/Alamy Stock
Photo; 15 TC Bird; 21 Daniela968/iStock; 22-23 Qulls/iStock;
25 TC Bird; 29 Andy Crawford; 33 Charlotte Cox; 36-37
Martina Litvinova/iStock; 39 Claire Richardson/narratives; 43
TC Bird; 47 Elizabeth Whiting & Associates/Alamy Stock
Photo; 51 Django/iStock; 62-63 Daniel Rudolf/iStock; 65 TC
Bird; 69 SIRIOH Co., LTD/Alamy Stock Photo; 75 TC Bird; 81
TC Bird; 84-85 subjug /iStock; 87 Anegada/iStock; 99
Bulgac/Getty Images; 106-07 TILLFX/iStock; 109 sassy1902/
iStock; 113 omgimages/iStock; 126 Charlotte Cox; 128 L
Charlotte Cox; R TC Bird

Front cover: Alamy SIRIOH Co., LTD/Alamy Stock Photo
Back cover: L: Claire Richardson/Narratives, C: Charlotte Cox,
R: TC Bird